wonder wheel

Sewanee Poetry

Wyatt Prunty and Leigh Anne Couch,
Series Editors

wonder wheel

poems   **Chelsea Whitton**

LOUISIANA STATE UNIVERSITY PRESS ▌▌ BATON ROUGE

Published by Louisiana State University Press
lsupress.org

LSU Press Paperback Original

DESIGNER: Barbara Neely Bourgoyne
TYPEFACES: Adobe Minion Pro, text; Carina Pro, display

Cover photograph: Colorized detail of *Butterfly's Tongue,* a photo-micrograph by
Arthur E. Smith, featured in Richard Kerr's *Nature Through Microscope and Camera*
(1909). Public Domain Image Archive.

LIBRARY OF CONGRESS CATALOGING-IN-PUBLICATION DATA
Names: Whitton, Chelsea author
Title: Wonder wheel : poems / Chelsea Whitton.
Description: Baton Rouge : Louisiana State University Press, 2026. |
    Series: Sewanee poetry
Identifiers: LCCN 2025045774 (print) | LCCN 2025045775 (ebook) |
    ISBN 978-0-8071-8587-2 (paperback) | ISBN 978-0-8071-8639-8 (epub) |
    ISBN 978-0-8071-8640-4 (pdf)
Subjects: LCGFT: Poetry
Classification: LCC PS3623.H5876 W66 2026 (print) | LCC PS3623.H5876
    (ebook) | DDC 811/.6—dc23/eng/20251124
LC record available at https://lccn.loc.gov/2025045774
LC ebook record available at https://lccn.loc.gov/2025045775

For my women.

contents

wonder wheel

The Mermaid Parade

Some gulls are circling my friends.
The ocean is a dull jade green.
Here comes the tall fin of a cycle.
Look how the Wonder Wheel rewinds.
We tip coconut rum into radiant
slush drinks, toast King Neptune

and the Mermaid Queen. Neptune
waggles his trident at my friends.
The Mer-Queen wears radiant
red anemones in her jade green
hair. The August air unwinds
my own pin curls. The cycle's

circling fin recedes, as cyclists
in silver suits flank Neptune's
roofless coupe—I pause, rewind
the memory, and find my friends
beside the clock. The jade green
ceiling of Grand Central's radiant

main concourse is still radiant
from wherever I am in this cycle,
before (or after) the jade green
surf divides for King Neptune,
divides me from my friends,
collapses time. Whoever winds

this clock, I think, must wind
the world itself. Even the radiant
Mer-Queen turns. Do my friends
fathom, yet, just what this cycle's
sharp fin means? King Neptune
comes before the jade green

flood. We put on jade-green
lipstick whilst the Q train winds
us deeper into Brooklyn. Neptune
meanwhile, rides time's radiant
fin in a sesquicentennial cycle.
When the parade ends, my friends

blow jade-green kisses at the radiant
blushing boy who winds the Cyclone.
Neptune rises. I will miss my friends.

part I

The Tiger

I like the tiger best. Big claws
that flex, dig into the invisible
flesh of morning. It is already
too hot. I like the tiger. He is
beautiful but he has got flies
all over his pretty gold eyes.
He looks so hot I want to go
inside his big glass cat house
and fan him like I was his
girlfriend. But, of course, he
would never have me. How
many women must come by
each day and beg to be his
woman. He says, *You like me
belly-up and heat-drugged.
You love me with seven inches
of glass between us. Your lot
gets hot looking down from
the mezzanine, tossing a steak.*
I stammer. Tiger, I say, I'm
a poet. I can love you better
than those other girls. I'll tell
the world your story, tell them
all how hot you are. You'll be
my muse. I'll make you live
forever. *Quite an offer,* he says
panting. *Can I eat you after?*

Initiation with Miter Saw

I want you to show me where to put my hands
in this garage of bug-specked pegboard,
innumerable boxes of parts. Near where the old
red stain—blood sacrifice or antifreeze,
symmetrical as a Rorschach lobster—
bifurcates the floor. I want to be shown,
your hands over mine, how to keep
the wood steady; how not to jump three feet
when the saw roars alive; how to rip it
irrevocably. My hands hate to commit. They prefer
half-measures, are in the cool habit of gripping
things loosely. They especially shrink from
what can't be undone. I want to know how
one earns it, this nerviness. If there's a badge
for follow-through, I want to see where you
keep yours. Is it shelved down here,
in the box marked *parts,* or is it upstairs,
folded into your bedside book,
along with a note from your father?
I'd like an idea of the standard procedure.
How close must one come to the actual blade?
Does a held breath help? Would you call it
a mostly forgettable experience? How bad
would it be if I just closed my eyes?
I want only to have already done it.
To be already holding the separate halves.

My Lover's Wife

My lover's wife is unlike me—she goes
like a fine green trick of the light,
her hair disarranged with begonias
and ballpoint pens. I bought her book.

It isn't as pretty as she is—at least
that is what all men say. Anyway, I
haven't read it. I just carry it around
to get it dirty. I had a dream I Sphinxed

my lover's wife—I mean I riddled her
and whipped her with my tail. It was as
erotic as a coffin turning over. I did
not have enough gin for her bath.

Her skin, burnt carbon in the dream,
that tonic smell of forms in triplicate!
I woke up coughing like an engine.
If I became my lover's wife, I would

not be as pretty as my lover's wife.
I think, *If I could kill her*—I could
never kill her, though I should, for she
has taken fire from August, has unmade

a thing I loved—*if I could kill her,*
splash the bottle-green of her with
pitch, I think, *the light would go to*
someplace else, would not be left to me.

Millennialogue, 2014

At any streetcorner the feeling of absurdity
can strike any man in the face.
—ALBERT CAMUS

So, here's me pitching myself
into an obsolete phone booth
on a busy intersection of hats
and mustaches, and everybody
here is bored to tears and skin
and bones, and we are all on
time. We are all making time
for a little belligerent pigeon-
kicking behavior. Depressed,
or so frustrated we can't even
breathe correctly? Me, I'm like
a cat that's been tricked into
a horrible sweater. Trees leer
and flash their green at me.
I barely tell anybody. Tell me
about yours. Don't stop. Your
special heat? I'm listening but
I'm not really listening. I *am*
listening but lately something
isn't right. What is this drear
that keeps us coughing into
morning? I'll tell you, *I don't*
feel well. I'll tell you, *I'm still*
not so hungry I'll eat anything.

O Shit Show

What will they call this fiasco
when we are gone, ourselves
unable to address this world
we know: these Day-Glo flowers,
haunted houses, shoe-strung
powerlines; these chords and
colors we love flung together,
how we dance and speak and
cut our hair, those gemstones
we adore, this flair, that ore,
the mostly perfect metaphor
of water, which we treasure
and pollute without excessive
care, coastlines and lake lands,
rivers where we weep and play,
these fish, these bugs, these
trees, these weeds, this list of
breeds we tolerate, this list of
so-called pests, the looks we
give each other over what we
eat for breakfast, listening as
always to news, this news, our
news, which sings and wails in
streaks and rivulets across our
airplane views, our news, which
must one day be history, which
must one day be folklore, our
poor, old, woe-begotten internet,
the glory holes punched through
our haze, the peepshow of our
slippage over what we used to
worship into what we hope one
day to fuck, but also *what* keeps
sneaking up on us, bombing our

selfies, stealing tithes, buying up
the munitions, burrowing into
our best descriptions of what
hell's boss wants with those—
not us!—who are bound for its
flames, *what* is in our costumes
and blue checks, our roiling
currencies, our separated text-
necks and jaw pains, each trigger
finger shoved into gloves we got
crocheted bespoke by weeping
robots, whilst our Pup Cups
runneth over, whilst we breach
like ring-lit shipwrecks, heirloom
daydreams sunk by cartoon-fast
reactors with code-generated
nicknames whose hot pics of
justice mix with pics of fresh-
plucked shame like so much
brackish water, hitting pixelated
falls that tumble every story
of the future we've been sold
into retelling: froth of every
shelling, pus from every plague,
loose hair from every braid
in which we placed a hopeful
plait—unwound, absorbed like
every pound of fat we bet would
make a difference lost or gained
—gone anyway, now, ravaged
or raveled, spun or rearranged,
just viscera, this blood and gore
we call a discourse, nothing less
or more. Maybe our best hope is

ahistory, that whatever comes after
this won't know how bad it got.
Maybe they'll call our war stains
spilled fruit pulp. Maybe they'll
even whistle something optimistic,
                mopping it all up.

Summer in the City

The city goes bug-eyed on me, in the unripe-
persimmon sour of Independence Day. I send

my body home in shimmers, only ever barely
where I am along the way. It is so hot, the sky

so low and soaking, I think maybe all of these
people in their coils and queues are rags around

a torch about to go up. I am delivering myself
unto a darkened room, a bed, a forest overgrown

with photocopies, not to be disturbed. I swerve
instead into a karaoke bar. I talk myself into

a happy hour. I sing "Purple Rain" and "Landslide"
to the pulled-down shades. The park was a mess

and I was sad on you again, so I got good and
day-drunk. Took in a magnum of cheap white

and gave myself a headache. Bit my tongue
so hard I nearly choked. I wanted somebody

to notice me, loud as I could, dividing my own
cells beneath an elm tree, spitting blood, painting

the moss red, laughing hard. I was so mad
at you, and mad for madness' sake, and mad,

of course, at my own sloppiness. I had to lie down.
Looking up, I thought what sheer, pathetic narcissism

it must take for the moon to show her cratered face
in daylight, to lodge herself like shrapnel in the side

of a middle-aged sky with a million problems probably
worse than her own. I was mad at the squirrels, too.

Allowed to spar in open air—no fear of causing pain,
or of lust coming into their game, messing everything up.

But *there's a place for us, / Somewhere a place for us*—
I sing it like Natalie probably did, before they gave that up

and dubbed her. I am wondering, with sloe gin sloshing
on the stage, if this is now the worst place I have been.

I'd thought the park would have a fountain. Thought I'd sit
along the edge and watch my feet turn into fish and swim off.

But there was never going to be a fountain. It was not
that kind of park and I was not in charge of my own feet.

One minute I was belly-up and spinning, muddy sunlight
sawing gently at my gag reflex. The next, I'm making

Patsy Cline do cartwheels in her grave and thinking, *Maybe
I am actually crazy.* Maybe you are right now drowning

in a lake. It makes no difference. I've already carved
your name into the underside of everything. Unique

New York. I love this place. I do. It is pulling out my
innards so much faster than my usual taxidermy.

I really am much lighter than I used to be. I've shaped
myself into a grand Manhattan blasphemy. Dead eyes

and soft, immobile wings. Like everybody. Pretty,
pointless things. Before I leave I must remember to

replace my ring. I don't feel much like singing anymore.
I'll let the city do the final act without me. I am indisposed.

After this drink, I really must be making my way home.

On Friendship

You, in a hot-pink tube dress.
You, with the ten thousand objectives.
You, whom I loved unreservedly. You,
who touched my face and called,
through pouted lips, my dun skin porcelain.

Our girl-group's Dean Moriarty.
Scheherazade of best nights ever.
I dreamed you in a bell jar filled with whiskey;
dreamed us old together, our long hair silver,
soft as eider, knit with promise rings.

You, whom I lost to the summer, to hands
moving under the table, where I couldn't see them.
Would you believe me if I told you
from this distance you look
like a doomed spare bird? Just like a bird.

I would have you fixed and illuminated,
framed inside a diorama of contented burden-beasts.

You, I would take to the movie of happiness.
I would tell you that warmth is not a cinematic treatment;
it is the grease-and-brine coat of ordinary living,
it is the smoke from what will burn up, either way.

Bless This

Mess, I swear—

By the stars, by the moon's black taffeta veil,
by the bend in the peafowl's half-hourly wail,
by the kitchen door stoop, by my grass-
covered feet, by the vibrating windows,
the dropping of bass, as a souped-up sedan
makes its showboating way down the street,

by the zigzagging lamps, by my overnight eyes,
by my nails chewed to nubs, by the Saturday
chap in my thighs, by the stamp from the club,
by the last cigarette in a pack I quite possibly
stole, by my chattering teeth, by the blood
on my knees, by my palpable lack of control,

by the trouble I've set like a trap, by the creak
in the door—on my life, I don't want anymore.

Child's Pose on the M34

Summon a rose, a ring, a rocket,
pocketful of kid noise saved for

years. It's time to find it. Follow its
memory, the finest good thing you

can think of . . . Oh, but who knows
what to do with it right now, in this

place, anyway? Your hopes are spent.
You felled them yourself, too soon,

like timber obelisks inscribed with
your beginnings, glyphs laughed at,

deemed too sentimental, wanting.
Isn't this why you're now burning up?

There's nothing old enough in you to
cast a shadow, lend you shade in which

to stand. You'll tell your children,
if you have some, that an axe is a weapon

forever, even in its sleep. Right now,
asleep inside its stump in Carolina,

you bet yours is dreaming, bloodily,
of laying waste. You dreamt of mice, once:

three. The third mouse spoke to you.
She felt oracular, stood upright and apart

from her twin brothers, each of whom
just hunkered rattily, their eye-beads

as alert as hers were soft with tear flow.
Let the wind blow, she said, maybe. Or

she said: *Let them go.* You don't know
why such nonsense sticks with you, only

that the seeing she-mouse can't be you,
not as you are now, doubled, head against

the window of this smelly uptown bus,
in such a mood. You have half decided

to forget the word *sublime.* You are so
tired of looking, tired of sucker punches,

gutted shock and awe. Are you marooned
up here, glib sun irradiating everything alike,

tinfoil flashing like ore on every sidewalk?
Baby, you've strayed too far uptown.

Nobody here is going to help you down.

Elegy for an Ex-Cat

Your cough
became our reveille, inciting
a daily sideways sprawl, sheets
flying, birdfeeder
outside the window knocking.

And while we
spun records and drank wine
from plastic cups, you lay,
sphinx cast in bronze, tasting
the hairs on your forearms.

You spent evenings
by the baseboard stunned,
spitting at our mutiny—
the sudden juts,
our sweeping limbs.

And in the midnight white
silence of fans and stilted
breathing, I know I saw you,
dark and soft-lined, blinking
morse code at me
with your light-trap eyes.

It is not that I miss
your unscrupulous hiss
or those quick, petty swats.
All that senseless, ceaseless
bathing; your great, wet
slobbering strokes.

Least of all I miss
the way you hated me

dispassionately. As if you
couldn't be bothered
to commit to loathing.

As if you knew
I'd soon enough be
nobody to you, or to him.

I've grown accustomed to
the rise and shrink of
shadows passing, night black
through my days. How
strange of yours to yearly
lengthen, following the sun.

Our Fancy Bonsai Tree

is curling like a prophet's wizened smirk,
into itself, its leaves and branches frying
in a murder bath of sun, and we confess
to ourselves that we don't love it anymore,
that we don't want it now. It is so ugly,
so deranged by heat and inattention, we
cannot recall its former feeling. We cannot
picture it unravaged. So beloved was it,
for all of seven seconds, that we threw
away those kitschy satin flowers. Kept since
college, unpacked and repositioned in kitchen
after kitchen—we remember *them* clearly,
the red and blue pansies with glitterized leaves,
the real-feathered ghost of a finch on a stick,
lacquered fruit. False arrangements are better,
we figure, just now. There is no bad faith in
their drooping. We can re-bend their stems
a thousand ways to suit our thousand moods.
Whereas this tree, so longed for in a moment
of whimsy, leaned one way every day, only further.
It was all too real for us. Indifference grew
like mildew. We "forgot" to water it, "forgot"
to read that pruning pamphlet. Left it to waste
in the blaze of our August kitchen until someone
stuck a Post-it note of mercy to its one, warped limb:
Please throw me away. And so today we wrap a bag
around its wretched shape and ask forgiveness.
Not for torturing the tree, but for believing
we could buy our own transcendence,
discount, at the boutique hardware store.

Companion

At dusk, you carve the table legs into
clawed feet. I keep track of the sawdust,
jarring it for future uses yet unknown. I'd like
to carve a creature of my own someday.

Meanwhile, I've covered up for you.
I have done up the tough white buttons
at my wrists and throat. I hope you notice,
and I hope you let me have a sip of that.

Your neighbor called to talk about
the field behind your house. He says
your land is just unhappy. It wants to be
called fallow, not infertile, from now on.

I want you to forget, someday, that I am
not your woman. I want to wear your overalls
and ride the swinging gate. Sometimes I come
into your room and you don't make me leave.

Tonight the stars are clean.
You sharpen wooden claws and whistle.

I make dark tea and file my nails, stand by
the screen door waiting for someday to come
like a beast running fast through the empty
field you still pretend you do not own.

Le Mauvais Objet

Be even my heaven commanded

but I could never help it so damned

odd was I so damned irregular and

angular and big and also too small

too florid and floor-eyed and fuzzy-

headed, fever-faced and flushed

and full of crap and I could dress

like something upright and imbibe

wine blandly like the photonegative

of someone's bride but I could never

give a traditional blush for decorum's

sake and as such had no real feel for

getting inspected, for sitting still

while being stroked and searched

and told about myself. So heaven

made me give them back: all those

charming descriptors, my unanimous,

handsome unbeauty. *So what?* I said.

The truth is nothing sun-spun sticks

around past sundown unless someone

sticks it down. Truth is most truths are

cabbages for compost, pound for pound.

A Few More Lines for the Torturer's Horse

with Auden and Bruegel

There is a contradiction in the darkened barn
where your tack hangs—stirrups and halters,
stainless bits, hoof trimmers, forceps, buggy
whip, iron hooks like little violent moons,
the scythes of lesser gods. These tools of upkeep,
ownership, and care have near-twin siblings,
hung up elsewhere, used for different purposes.
But you don't know this, horse. His tools are
innocent, easily cleaned and put away,
and every inch as unaccountable as you were
the first day your master hitched you
to a doomed man's jerking limb. And afterwards,
he washed you gently, rinsed your hide until
the water ran off clear—not red, or red and brown.
He rubbed you down, called you a good horse,
cleaned your teeth and picked the rocks out
of your shoes. He whistled *Darling Clementine*
and led you out to graze beside your favorite tree.
He used his tools that day in ways that made you
love him. Horse, I know how you love him:
hopelessly, as any kept thing loves whatever
is most merciful to it. And this is innocence itself,
and you are blameless in your love of his warm hands,
coarse as they are, against your withers, teasing
clots of blood out of your tangled mane.

part II

Four Harbingers

Hecate

of the crossroads and of undecidability,

of no-moon nights that spoon-bend reason,

acid laughter leaking from an awful place

Athena

of motherlessness and queer-born girlhood,

of gray-eyed clapbacks, of upshots delivered,

insight ripping from behind like owl talons

Demeter

of the bitter bargain, of the doubled-over grief

of mothers granted hell-shaped mercy, of hand-

biters and blight-bringers, never quite the same

Hestia

of forgotten labor, silent all-mother to legions

of servants, of lives boiling over in back rooms,

their hymns bleached of words yet humming still

The Queen Mother

Death's children
Resemble you and me
—CHARLES SIMIC

I.

My babies borrow hunger from their mother.
They are legion. They are saltwater pearls.

I hate the pretty ones more than the others.
This is not their fault. Not really. All my girls,

they wear my names like cast-off cameos.
They walk the earth. Their footsteps make it shake

and roil. They do my bidding where they go,
explosively. I braid the sounds they make

into a crown. Gone from me now, my clones,
my children. Off to blot the wide world out.

I sleep my days in and sit nights alone,
reading their leaves. I scry their whereabouts.

How wide their eyes must be, like riverbeds.
My fingers twitch whenever they have fed.

II.

They feed on sulfur, red dust, smog. Hard-pressed,
a tailpipe's pickled spew. Their teeth are black

with the sweet of their mayhem, rotted through.
I check up on them. Mother needs contact.

They send me postcards from each new address,
but rarely take my calls, and when they do

it is all screams and lies. I've raised them right.
I feel their love, unhinged and gladly cruel,

and I return it. Feed them silence. Dare
each one to cry. Their laughter is my fuel.

They torture one another, bathe in spite
and line their eyes with wanton disrepair.

I've made them in my image after all
I say, pulling my knife out of the wall.

III.

I pull my knife out of the wall and gasp
at the incision's depth. My strength returns

a little more each day. I feed their curse
news clippings, mostly. Watch its blue flames yawn

and take their due. It eats what's passed.
I comb the cinders, tenderly. Unburned

remains are rendered to my devil's purse
to spend as currency. My girls are gone

and can't return, but one day they may ask
for intercession. What little they earn

won't buy them amnesty. I'll reimburse
the stars. Outfit them with new fates. Un-pawn

their cameos. Return them to the streets.
It's understood that Mother dines on meat.

IV.

I dine on meat, most of it carrion.
Roadkill pan-seared, a glass of sauvignon—

grapes of my wrath, pulverized by their feet.
Distilled for centuries, it tastes quite sweet.

Each dish I primly garnish with the wan
white skulls of songbirds, savory as prawns.

(Birds were my children, too, not long ago.
I honor them, devouring them. They know.)

I take most meals alfresco, with the Moon.
We talk about our children, toast their ruin

and rebirth. I am quite drunk by morning.
My good Moon leaves me a sober warning:

Like you, they cannot stop once they've begun.
Take care to hide our daughters from the Sun.

V.

To hide my daughters from the Sun, I cloak
them in disguises. Nothing so banal

as wigs and false mustaches. No such smoke.
I build them bodies, give them words to call

their earth anatomy. Habits and ticks
to blur them with the pink neurotic herd.

Humiliation and unease, I trick
them into swallowing. The little birds,

their hunger blinds them to my sabotage.
They need these weaknesses to fool the light

of day. I teach them the deformed dressage
of modesty, and how to mimic fright.

This way, they walk in sunlight undetected,
become quite powerful and well respected.

VI.

I was once powerful and well respected
in my sphere. Some say I was a sphere

myself, when all this was new. I never
held that title in my time. Whatever

you've heard, if you have, overestimates
my influence, I assure you. Create

and destroy. These were jobs I accepted
with no small solemnity, many tears.

It's amusing, I suppose, to have cried
at the beginning. Strangely terrified,

I was, of taking the first swipe. Cold feet
as they say. It was childish. Indiscreet.

Some looking back is to be expected.
No small abandonment has left me here.

VII.

I leave them—you know who—in open fields,
on doorsteps, bassinetted by the wind,

to squall until the good people reveal
themselves, take pity, take my babies in.

And bad babies they aren't—babies are
disposed to bursts of cruelty as a rule.

No, they develop naturally as far
as parents know. Already making fools

of the habitually good, they grin
like angels, giggle, shriek at peek-a-boo.

The cuckoo lays her egg among strange kin
and leaves it there. It hatches, ousts its few

faux siblings from the nest, and mother wren—
nine times in ten, she doesn't know who's who.

VIII.

Who's nine-tenths a woman? Who is almost
a perfect specimen, apart from freak

unaccountables? Stepping on a crack,
who still thinks of her mother? Like a ghost,

whose mother overrides her thoughts to speak
of tidiness, good posture, judgment day?

Who knows the most slimming color is black?
Who holds her shame like a pearl in her cheek?

Whom can a man make happy? Who can say
where her happiness lies? In a glove, left

behind on the winter playground? A dime
too deep to dive for? Something about play?

Who is all grown up now? Who can tell time?
Who straddles the crack for an hour, bereft?

IX.

Each hour's a crack-up I straddle, bereaved.
Time licks its chops. I pace the littered floor.

I've never been much good at waiting for
gratification. What my children leave

when they are finished isn't very much.
I boil their leftovers to make thin soup.

I pace the floor, repeat myself, and touch
the darkness. Play at pining. Play, on loop,

their lives like lava flows. Each violent birth,
the subsequent destruction. Falling trees,

the screams of men. Whole cities on their knees.
Again. Again. And yet, each time, the earth

resets. Each time my girls make something new.
They inch toward midnight. It is what they do.

X.

This is what we do: we inch the big hand
back a minute each hour. It's anxious work.

We are as canny as can be. You see,
if mother ever caught us near her clock—

well, penance is one word for it. Mama
would not be pleased. So, we do it this way:

One sister diverts her with a big, planned
mess. Two others throw tantrums, go berserk

in tandem, split her energies. Some three
or four of us keep watch at the door, knock

five times when the orchestrated drama's
at sixes and sevens; eight, when the melee

is peak. The bravest, careful of the chime,
makes sure that it is never quite bedtime.

XI.

Sleep comes for all. Make no mistake. I am
no warmed-up euphemism. I'm that which

devours. Yes, sweet baby, I am that witch
of the bone claw, rapping nightly. I am

why you spit over your shoulder. I am
what you spit on. It doesn't matter which

harbinger you believe in: I'm that witch
and I will eat you up. But first, I am

a mother. I invent the sky, bloom light
into it. Knit the molecules for air

and tear new life out of the bleeding mud.
I am mother to rosehip and frostbite,

to pestilence, slow dancing, blues, warfare
and you. I built that need into your blood.

XII.

This bloody need to build a you and I
into the brickwork of cosmology,

to give it the stakes of a love affair,
to advance and retreat, to send letters

into orbit and stare hard at the sky
with a yearning that is frank, bodily,

and, heaven help you, real; to be aware
of dark matter and heat death, and fetter

yourselves to the mast anyway, like fools
—you are all fools, aiming radio waves

at infinity, begging *please, please, please,*
won't you let me, let me, let me—I've been

trying to let you. I've given you tools.
You have wasted your time on your knees.

XIII.

On our knees? Mother, please. Do you reckon
we bother to kneel? That we're beckoning,

expecting you to give us anything?
You confuse us with birds, with the many

penny-witted animals built to starve
in your wondrous lab. We have been carving

our names into the back of you, digging
away in broad daylight. If you must rig

the world to blow, we're going to get it while
we can. Don't reprimand us for smiling.

We look just like you, our own darling
progenitress. We've grown hard as the marl

we were born to, and as stiff. We don't bend
easily, and we rage at weak endings.

XIV.

I am weakening. Rage grips me easy
these days and temperance is a paper

bracelet. Soon I'll lose it altogether,
likely in the shower while weeping fire-

water. I am breaking open. I will
lift my eyes and see, above a choke

of trees, the feral sky, her tears of fleecy
ash. The lukewarm light of day will taper

down an unknown valley. Other weather
will be blowing in. I contain a pyre

inside me, built for this. Old as the hills,
it has been waiting for the perfect stroke.

Who has the flint to set the thing aroar?
My babies strike their matches on the floor.

part III

Productive Fallacies

My grandmother hated wind chimes.
She wouldn't accept the gift of one.
Said they sound like sadness, and I say

so, too. But I don't hate them. After all,
I don't hate winter, don't hate last year's
empty bird's nests, or those ancient koi

iced into Brooklyn's fountains. I know
fish aren't sad themselves. They only
take my sadness into them, away

from me. They only strap it to their
piebald backsides, bear it winter long.
Their bellies drag the pond scum floor

in slow, cold circles with or without
the additional weight of my sadness.
They aren't sad. They nibble last year's

water lily root and dream of spring.
I'm from where loblolly pines line
coastward highways. Scab-skinned

and too tall, tough as weeds, they loom
like cursed men. They look like sadness.
They look like they're damned to live

forever lonely, all together, set apart
like an unhappy family. But I know
they aren't unhappy. If they do feel

anything, it's pride. They've struggled
and survived. Now, they drink first
when the clouds part. They have earned

their patch of sky. Still, the raw-eyed
sight of them rips sadness out of me
at sixty miles per hour, rain or shine.

I could not contain it if I tried. I have.
I've tried it thirty times. Fifteen vacations
come and gone along that sun-bombed

highway. The loblollies get to me every
time. Not so with wind chimes. I went
six whole months and didn't mind my own

at all. Their mingled voices, minnow-
bright, sent my contentment back to me
like silver balls. Last night, after your call,

I got the hammer out and flattened them
one by one, against the dead stone wall.

When I Am Involved with You

lately, I come
to nothing much

softness of very
crumpled paper, crumbs
of undevourability, which,
sprinkled throughout
our wedding bedding, are not
constellated, constituted
into dough, not leavened
with your breathing,
with its candy-eating
sweetness, tongued
as I have been by
metaphor, tasted
by science, masticated

by your eyes,
your eyes
the eyes of all of you,
your clever selves at once—my love,

as such, I feel
more you than me, lately,

am neither
viaduct nor valley, neither
callow nor burlesque—*I never did*
offend you in my life!

—I am being
as real as can be—

but love, I'm rather,
really, lately, like
a bag of Wonder
crumbs saved up
for hungry birds.

I'm really rather
lately like a crumpled
newspaper whose
language runs
in any kind of rain.

Southerners and Hurricanes

How much can our walls retain until they simply seem?
And what if what we say they are belies us? What if
walls are lies? Two things we say we understand
completely: walls and lies. We do not shudder, shutter up
the windows yet. A storm is coming, candles out—
two things we understood, even in dreams. And where
were you? And where were yours when the very light fled?
I was somnambulant. My years of tossing groomed me
for this passage. And still I was frightened, though not
of the things I felt I understood: my love of existence,
its tenuousness, my lost blowing past like such loose trash,
like weeds, the ghosts of summer, their green bones bared.
Loss and music—two things one may come to
understand. Everything leaves. Acquire an ear for it.

Contralto

for Patsy

A fever burned your baby voice to char
at thirteen, smoked it holy, taught you young
to spin pain into dark silk. Any scar
can be polished. Any song can be sung

down an octave. Any name can be yours
if you're willing to give up the old one.
The voice was wise, was womanly before
your first heartbreak, before you had begun

to sing a woman's song. Before you made
the jukebox cry—*I fall to pieces*—notes
like honeyed tears; before it ever paid
to be a doll with the blues in her throat.

You wore rodeo fringe and sang for fun.
Your voice was like a bruised, blue plum.

Dear June

(1929–2003)

I mouth your barbed-wire melodies
by candlelight, believing I'm smoke

in the rafters of the bars where you
crowed. I lean into the long notes,

the ones that bend like begging, full
of thirst. I do not wonder what you

are so thirsty for. And June, the way
you grip the notes as if with fists, as if

that swallerin' place might never come—
that breathlessness, that same caged

effort rings out nightly in the reams
of conifer behind my home. I wonder

some at your final performance. Pretty
ghost, you left us hungry. You went out

with eyes like thunderclaps, unsmiling,
only halfway humble, not quite tearful,

nodding at some distant drunken rumble,
your voice understated, crystalline

and fine, an heirloom ribbon pulled
loose one more time. Dear June, I lose

you following the light out of the day,
and find you young and wiry, wrapped

around your autoharp, suntanned
and river-ruddy, happy, flashing teeth.

After Moonrise

She is great,
We measure her by the pine-trees.
    —H.D.

We still have a song.

It has been years
since the banks were this
narrow. The water does
come back to us,
after all.

We measure her. She is
over there, under
that pine-tree, so small
we mistake her light
for one of ours.

It has been years since we danced.

Will you glimmer
now that we are looking
up again? Will you only
blink on us, forgetting us?
We were great once.

Now we measure
ourselves by our own
thinnesses. O flight—
we are still singing
—swing us swiftly

back around again.

Panic

What scree, what gnashed bray,
loosed, through the goat-boy's teeth
from the trees, from between
the tight young boles of saplings
—a burrowed source: the botched
faun not like the rest of those so easy
going in their vinous ramblings, good-
time goblins piping for a lucky toss.
This other one, tetched and off-kilter,
nurses other predilections. This one
quickens at a scream. Aberrant
satyrling, our cloven sadist's whistle
only wets for dread. What warp
of creation bleats unaccountable
clamor from a nowhere thicket?
You know him. We all do. His brand
is chaos. His flute lifts when the back
is turned. His din wants your safety
to curdle, wants your rising sickened,
that acid purchase in the throat's
trapdoor. From dampened hollows,
his freak flute draws out a hircine fug
that's nothing like the loamy excrete
of arousal, unlike anything except
itself: fear sweat. He cannot get
enough of it. Oh little sicko, billy-
kid, *dost thou not know who made
thee?* Cursed ugly by feckless sires?
Or is he only homely in a province
run by gods and nymphomaniacs?
In any case, the chase has spoiled
his wardrobe, made him messy. We
see through his T-shirt, see he's just

another backseat bogie, bridge troll
with a vegetarian secret: All his big
bad clatter, all those droning strings
portending any-second doom are
hollow bottles, noisome garbage,
mere wind bothering a stand of reeds.

Selected Nightmares

Sometimes the good guy goes off script, goes
evil, and an unsheathed hunting knife appears
between you on the kitchen table. It is so out
of sync, so funny, that you don't reach for it,
don't react in time, but he does, and the wind
picks up. Sometimes you draw your fist back,
move to make a break for it, and . . . nothing.
Nothing. Sometimes you are driving along
a familiar road, not paying much attention,
and a sinkhole opens wide in front of you.
You're always going far too fast to stop. Don't
bother trying out the brakes. They never work.
Sometimes your mom is in the car with you.
Sometimes she's screaming. Sometimes she is
standing in the road between the sinkhole
and your brakeless, speeding car. Sometimes
a huge, panting composite of your top five
scary dogs is real and chasing you. Sometimes
you feel its breath against your legs. You feel
your flesh tear in its teeth. Sometimes you kick it
and it morphs into the kind of dog you'll feel
ashamed of kicking later. Sometimes you are
falling from the sky. Just falling from the sky.
You don't recall the fatal flaw that sent you
falling from the sky, but you are yellow with
remorse for it—so sorry!—as you fall forever,
certain you will die. Sometimes you *are* dying,
slowly, of mysterious diseases. Sometimes
you feel fine and only guess that you must be
dying because people keep buying you flowers
and telling you they love you. Sometimes a filthy
clown emerges from the woods and you are
quite alone and miles from anybody's birthday.

Sometimes you are pregnant. Often, you are
pregnant. Sometimes the father is a succubus
demon, but not usually. Usually, he's a friend
of yours who's not your husband. Or better yet,
he is your husband's friend. Occasionally, you do
get lucky and it's only aliens. They only want to
cut your baby out and raise it to be David Bowie.
(This is not a real nightmare. Please see Selected
Delusions of Grandeur.) Sometimes you're pregnant
with a loaded gun. Sometimes you give birth to a son
and he comes at you with a loaded gun. Or else
he looks just like your mother when he screams.
Or else he looks just like the little dog you never
meant to kick that day in grade school. Or else
you have been hopelessly wrong about everything,
all this time. You only thought that you were pregnant,
but you see it now. You are still falling from the sky.

Poseidon

A far-flung sky, a coast, a nape of thorns. This ocean lives two lives
at once; it has a struggle in it. You want to be thought dangerous and
so you learn to swear. The kids raised here go north or they are never
happy. Weddings happen all the time but never has there been a fiftieth-
anniversary party here. It is said that your eyes were as blue as shallow
water when they named you; they are darker than the deepest trenches
now. Your mother pays you twenty dollars to unclog the gutters. You
buy a radio and lash it to a rafter in the back shed where you spend
most school days, lying in a hammock you liberated from one of the
empty summer homes your mother cleans. A girl in your class named
Sara gives you airplane bottles of tequila and weed when she can. In
exchange you pretend to be her boyfriend around her parents, and give
her rides in your stepfather's truck, out to her real boyfriend's trailer
inland. All the trees here are dry, scabby pines or else they are imported
from somewhere else to make the town look beachy. All the men here
are either work-broken or leisure-ruddy. Both kinds wear boat shoes and
keep their shirts untucked. They love to spit into the sea. For your part,
you are almost always lying wasted in your shed. Or else you are mowing
the lawns of the rental properties, listening to NOFX on your Discman,
watering their gated gardens, maintaining their private dunes. It is said
that your mother named you Poseidon when she first looked into your
pools of eyes but later changed your name to something sensible when
she couldn't sleep for dreaming of your death. Knee-deep on a squall
day, she would find herself facing the ocean, singing to the bundle in her
arms. Then, from the deep, an improbable riptide would grip her, shift
the sand and she'd be taken under. Your pink shape would slip free of her
swaddle, would pull out fast and fast to sea. She would invariably wake
up screaming. She took some pills. She gave up coffee, gave up chili, slept
with one quick hand inside your crib. And still the dream, each night, the
same ending, until she changed your name to Steve and left your father.

Squally Day in East Rock

The view's still troubled, driving
    into town. Hysterical trees,
as big as buildings, buffet and roil
    in the wake of an all-night storm.
We see the green-black bluff,
    the tree line crawling like a cat's
arched back, and we are all
    grown up now—we've known
storms, we are initiated—but we,
    I think, are each a little frightened
of this foam-lipped landscape. Still,
    your truck is teal and weatherproof
and warm. Still, we smoke a joint
    and tune the radio. And when
you sing along with Peter, Paul
    and Mary *I'd ring out danger, I'd*
ring out a warning!—I do believe
    you would. Our voices, cracked
and dappled as New England clapboard,
    do not tremble. This, you teach me:
Nothing touches us. You make this day,
    this drive, look easy. Look at
what you've rendered from your
    second life, foraging daily for
usable light. You pick it, piecemeal
    from the brambles of this strange
dim town. Already on neighborly
    terms at the hardware store,
where you bought paint last month,
    stayed on to moderate a neighborly
debate over birdseed. One man said
    he likes to sprinkle seed along his
windowsills, right after it snows, in case
    some of the birds need time to say
goodbye, to settle their affairs, to go.

The other men thought such largesse
ridiculous, and said so, but you understood
    him perfectly. Tomorrow, you'll show
me the ten-pound bag of WILD BIRD
    FOOD slumped over in the mudroom,
waiting for the year's first snow. Today,
    we're here to buy bleached twine,
a small, clawed hammer—*If I had a hammer*—
    and a box of one-inch nails. The shop
is stocked and tidy. Little piebald gourds
    for sale in baskets, THIS WEEK ONLY
specials on deep fryers and rock salt.
    The air's a friendly twist of cedar, fresh-
brewed coffee, turpentine, and dirt.
    Month's end, Ed says, *we ought to be sold
clean out of shovels and Radio Flyers, but*
    —the rainfall hugs his pause—*business
was slow for Halloween, so who's to say?*
    We check the almanac: new moon,
precipitation. Driving home—your home
    I'm only visiting, still hunkered as
I am in busy Brooklyn, clinging, though
    it's getting cold, to summer's pretty
ghost; I am not ready, yet, to follow—you
    tell me about your latest project,
how you plan to build a makeshift loom.
    Twenty-four nails, two rows, with twine
zigzagged for heddles in between; ten feet
    a day of currant-colored yarn, over and
under; something called a clove-hitch
    knot. You say it'll take a month to do,
will be a little rug to go in your spare room.
    I'll be Penelope, you say, half laughing.
Peggy Seeger sings. I don't say anything.

Dad—

I don't think you knew who Elvis Costello was, but let's proceed

as if you did and do. You're loose dirt and white light now anyhow,

so let's say you know what I know. Okay, space ghost? Extra special

seldom-seen cicadas are upon us at the moment. They lurch out of

earth-holes like a prophecy. The folks on public radio will simply

not shut up about them. Brood X. Brood 10. Seventeen years in

in hypogeal limbo, now back with a vengeance, like Beetlejuice—

there's another reference you'd never have understood, oh well.

Each comes encased in a pearlescent amber shell which it then

shivers out of when the time is right, red-eyed and mostly black

with yellow racing stripes, big as a baby hummingbird, but dun

and graceless and benignly horrible, with crinkly wings the color

of a dirty ashtray. Still, I have to say I like them. They don't bite

or sting. They don't do anything but buzz about and hang out

in the dogwood trees. Bumbling and friendly, they remind me

of teenagers, which I guess they must be, given their fortnight

life span. One rode with me while I was working in the garden, clinging to my shoulder, croaking gently. But you'd know about

cicadas, even special, every-seventeen-years-rare cicadas. You knew

everything peculiar about local nature. Anyway, this has all been

to say we're out here, Matt and I, and the two cats. We're out

on our apartment's balcony, the one you called a too-high liability,

observing how the air is full of friendly little monsters; how they

drift across the foreground of our dropout view, on brand new wings

we know they'll only get to grapple with a few short weeks, and one

of us—I don't know who came up with it—started singing *watchin'*

the cicadas . . . watchin' the cicadas . . . get it? This delights us.

We are singing it now, as I write this. We've been sliding almost

absentmindedly into a kind of post-traumatic superbloom.

We are remembering the trick of resurfacing, exposing our interiors to sun.

Dad—

Just watched a speedboat rip a light-streak from a lake.

Just heard a loon keen, tucked my elbows back inside

a hammock-swing. Just popped a raspberry and tasted

purple, sweet and acid, hummed a little battle hymn,

undid my hair's taut night braid. You are only here

to hear me, now. I have you, wholly rapt, forever now.

Dad—

I plan to do a dead man's float until I gather enough

tools and scraps to build a raft. Thenceforth, I'll work

my oar, and fish, if there are fish. I'll try to notice

what I can about the world post-shore, and learn

to drift. Of course I'll be disoriented, lonely, but

I won't despair; I'll find the others. We'll collaborate,

form constellations, flow in webs and know

much more as one, the way a shoal knows when

to bend and where to go. We will cease dreaming

about hills and harbors—not because we won't

remember but because they won't arrive—and so

surviving, we will make new memories, invent

alternative cartographies. You asked me once why I

so seemed to like to fight. *Why don't you give that line*

a little slack? I was confounded by the question at the time.

Dad—

As a gift to both of us, I imagine you growing diffuse,

daily less like one thing, less a singular man, more like

a widening, a bloom, more room for outer space inside,

more time for listening, your life force like an ebb tide

now, returning to its making under moonlight, stirring

back into the star-works. I cannot wish it otherwise.

Spear Side / Patrilineality

/

Your lopsided father stuck
the loose stars to your sky
one summer. Even now
they glow up there as if,
like you, they are still dumbstruck
by the memory of his hulking grace.
With one foot on the bed, one on
the chest of drawers, his finger
pressed each phosphorescent
shard into eternity, too high
for anyone to tear them down.
It should have busted his ass
to do a thing like that. It did
—that kind of thing—eventually.

//

"That kind of thing, eventually,
will wear a man's skin thin," says mine.
His skin *is* thin, and mottled
from five decades in the sun,
on a vast green field that only winks
at abundance, that does not, in fact,
yield anything up, save little flags
from holes, the occasional sky-borne
alien egg. True enough, he's burned
his skin to paper for this game.
But he does not, this time, for once,
mean golf. He means grief. *That* kind
of thing. He means leaving a child
in the ground. All fathers suffer.

///

In the ground, all fathers suffer
the fate of the warrior. In life,
it's a sky of tin gods. Each one's
a private lodestar, lost to all but us.
Whatever they did for a living,
our dads, however they hustled
and failed, they spun silvery roses
from gum foil, and blew Vaudeville
tunes through grass kazoos. And when
they told us how it was, we listened.
We believed their tales were true.
And so, however rent and upside-down
and patched, we flew their flags
until everything real blew away.

////

Until everything real blew away,
your father's father's father raised
a subsistence of cabbages above
the fruited plain. *Nothing much
changed when the sky fell on us,*
it is said he is said to have said. Only
the high folks got knocked down.
Haha. What *could* bring a poor man
low, apart from winter? Every soul
piled in one bed with the newspaper
stuffed to plug leaks in the windows.
Still, to be survived by all six children!
His salt-blind headstone seems to read:
God is fair to the faithful who toil!

/////

God is fair to the faithful who toil.
Basically. Complicatedly. Squint
and try to see a version of events
in which good men are not heroic,
only good. Unmask that good
and you may find the face
of a previous father, not so
good. Meanwhile, and always,
and always without knowing why,
a procession of fathers stretches far
as infinity. Each one is in line to carve
his name over his father's name,
into the stone. It is only a stone,
but it shows them where to stand.

Harvest Song

after Bruegel

The world is wide, we say, and this is comforting
though perhaps it shouldn't be. We lie down
at day's end beneath this apple tree, or that one.

We try hard to love our families a little more
than strangers. We die in particular sick beds
behind the thick stone walls of homes we built

ourselves. We go. We go like field mice, we go
gently, we go quick or slow, but we all go, in rows
like golden fruit trees, yellow wheat. We go sheet

white and hope the night is friendly. We go knowing
that our kin will mow what's left to mow, and this
is also comforting. The world is wide. The world is

wider than we know. One cannot see the shape
of it from here below, but there are many rivers.
There are roads that must lead somewhere, surely.

Only we grow very tired by nightfall, ride the empty
hay cart down the hill to town in silence. Bullfrogs
crow from pondside hideouts. Vespers' bell toll beds

us down from just around those knolls. Some days
we dream of picking up and going for that plume
of smoke—that one on the horizon, wanly rising

into blue. Sometimes it is all that gets us through
this grueling scything, trying on the lithe life-suits
of strangers. We go riding off. We leave our work,

our husbands, wives still picnicking behind us. Leave
our children filthy, in their playclothes, shrieking
from a green patch. One day—we'd never want away

for any longer. Still, it's dangerous. The elders say
they don't come back that go that way, that wander
in dusk light, neglecting reaping. Better to lie down

in one's own mown meadow and be grateful for soft
ground. Far better knowing, going quietly, beloved,
than falling too soon from a sky we do not recognize.

Legendary

The little girls
Wove crowns
Of leaves
　　—SAPPHO

By an ancient, vine-warped yellow
house leaning into the valley's
rounded crest, we two grass-stained
daughters of summer endlessly rolled
the hill down to the hunching stream
with its narrow, lanky beds where
someone, sometime hid a honeydew
to cool against the wintry trickle.
By twilight, train whistles bleating
against the beveled laughter of
grownups gathered on the porch—
the sounds, swelling in the air, made us
go wild. Our bare feet swept across
the dimming field. In great green
circles we ran at top speed, drawing
wind from the still night air. Our voices
poured from us. We sang old, half-learned
hymns and chased the sun's bright rind
beyond the darkening blue ridge.

acknowledgments

Grateful acknowledgement is made to the editors of the following publications, in which the poems listed first appeared, sometimes in earlier versions or under different titles: *Atlanta Review:* "Our Fancy Bonsai Tree" and "Selected Nightmares"; *Bateau:* "The Tiger"; *Copper Nickel:* "Productive Fallacies"; *Cream City Review:* "Panic"; *Four Chambers:* "Dear June"; *Ilk:* "My Lover's Wife"; *Kindred:* "Southerners and Hurricanes"; *Petrichor Review:* "Companion"; and *Vinyl Poetry:* "On Friendship."

"A Few More Lines for the Torturer's Horse" was a finalist for the 2020 Adrienne Rich Award. "Harvest Song" appeared on the *Best American Poetry* blog. "Poseidon" was a finalist for *Southeast Review*'s 2024 Gearhart Poetry Prize. "Spear Side / Patrilineality" won the 2018 Sandy Crimmins National Prize for Poetry and was published in *Philadelphia Stories* (Spring 2018). "Summer in the City" appears in *Of Burgers and Barrooms* (2017), an anthology by *Main Street Rag*.

My deepest thanks to Wyatt Prunty and Leigh Anne Couch for selecting this collection to be part of their Sewanee Poetry series.

Thanks to Ellen Kochansky and the Rensing Center in Pickens, South Carolina, where I spent a month as poet-in-residence, wrote the first draft of "Spear Side / Patrilineality," and made friends with a goat.

Thanks to Sewanee University and the Sewanee Writers' Conference for your support and writing guidance.

Many thanks to my writing teachers, especially David Lehman, Catherine Barnett, Mark Bibbins, Craig Morgan Teicher, Jennifer Michael Hecht, John Drury, and Rebecca Lindenberg. Many of the poems in this collection began as drafts in your workshops, and I owe most of what I know about poetry to you.

Thanks to my writing co-conspirators, past and present, with whom I've shared a workshop table and/or living room floor. Yours are the eyes for which I wrote these poems. Especial thanks to Jess Smith, Lily Goderstad, Peter Burzynski, Sean Damlos-Mitchell, Christina Lancaster, Chelsea Reilly, Caitlyn Pezza, Brooke Ellsworth, Liz Axelrod, Roberto Montes, Katie Byrum, Mark Gurarie, Alex Crowley, Sakinah Hoffler, Madeleine Wattenberg, Sakinah Hofler, Corey Van Landingham, Kimberly Grey, Emily Rose Cole, Marianne Chan, Austen Allen, Lisa Low, Yalie Kamara, and Cara Dees.

Thanks to my oldest friends, my High Point-Greensboro-Asheville-Winston-Salem-Brooklyn-Queensand friends, the ones who remember the beginning. You know who you are. I love you!

This book is dedicated to my mother, who made me a poet more than anybody, and to my brilliant, inspiring sisters, Lindsay and Tammy. I love you.

All remaining credit and thanks go to Matthew Yeager, who loved this book into existence and without whom I would surely perish. Thank you for being my partner, and for our boys, and for everything else. I love you.